# Poetry Cured My Sanity

By: Daryl L. Hennix Jr.

ISBN: 978-0-6151-5813-6

*This Book is dedicated to my beautiful*

*little baby girl Neaveh who brightens*

*up every ounce of my days*

*Also to my grandfather who has*

*gone on before us.*

Thoughts beat my skull with
sledgehammers until they
bleed onto the pages I feed you
… Eat Up…

# CONTENTS

## 13 Going on 30

A painted face
Hides an inner fiend
That feeds on her
Pleasantries

Devours her smile
And drinks her
Milky joy

Role-models were
A thing of the past
Now she receives
Behavior advice via text message

The chatter of
A thousand voices
Persuade fashionable mutilation
Of the most pure of all
Canvases

What other course
Was she to travel?
What other choice
Was she given?
She wound up in intercourse
Of course

She often lay with
Men who have seen
A decade or more sunsets
Then she

The poison of
Drugs only encouraged
Her fiend to ravage
What's left of her innocents

I found her fully
Possessed by what
This evil media implanted

Abandoned young child
Clean off your face
Wipe off your knees and
Stand for me, be you,
Not them the child you are

## A Mothers Request to her Son's Demons

I've walked a mile on broken glass
Through charred coal and stinging ash
Opened up my scab healed wounds
Renounce worshiping the moon

I've swallowed sand to scar my throat
Left wet in the blizzard without a coat
Given insects feast of my flesh
Slaved for a millennium still with no rest

I supplied my blood for the stream
And left un-sown my skins seams
Freely slows what's left of me
My sacrifice
Please… "Let Him Be"

## All too Common Recipe

Add depression with pure sadness

Include life and extract all happenings of bliss

A dash of deceit

A teaspoon of daily struggle

And two cups of emotional pain

A tablespoon of heartache

A pinch of overwhelming stress

And let it sit till color seems plain

Stir with the magical power of hatred

And don't forget to add all of your fears

This is a recipe we all know all to well

The ingredients of tears.

## Any Second

Any second she will be walking through the door

Any second we'll be playing the game

NO I LOVE YOU MORE

Any second she'll be telling me exactly how her day

went

And we'll laugh and joke about how her time was

spent

Any second she'll come in and we'll stand and smile

at each other

And when we go to bed I'll thank God that I found

another

Any second she'll come in as she has every other

day

I've been here standing so long I can't accept that

you passed away

## Azul

If I ever needed
You before, I need you now.
My sanity has been
Victimized for the
Last time.

Walk with me, not
For me, hand and hand
Through the place
Where my thoughts command
All you see.

Where Azul impregnates
My fertile imagination
And gives birth to creatures
Not of our realm

Step into my mind
To witness your
New lifelong nightmares

I need your strength
Please don't forsake me
I've turned back for the
Last time

His ghouls will
Frighten me no longer
With you by my side

Brave with me my lakes
Of loneliness
No matter the depths
Or waves

Climb with me
My mountain of lies
Despite the boulders
I used you to create

Stand along side me
While I stare, Azul
Into his charcoal
Black eyes

Be there for me
While I command my
Demon to release my
Soul

And trust me when I say
To you that I have changed

## It's Beautiful

It's beautiful isn't it the way the water reflects the
sun?
And the white capped hill in the horizon and the
mountain beyond that one.
The way the leaves float on the breeze and in turn
get carried away.
And when the wind blows the stern trees agree that
they'll sway.

Isn't it beautiful the way the fields of green go on
for miles at a time?
Unbroken by the pavement unwilling to bend to the
modern times
Standing and holding steadfast in their ways
Take a moment to glance before the end of our days

Isn't it beautiful the way the ocean seems to fold
into its very own pride?
And even the organisms within take it for a ride
How it is that something so vast enters ones mind so
infrequently
Yet has the power to end my sights not respecting
its entirety

Isn't it beautiful the way that the sun sets in the late
afternoon?
As it fades away from the mountains the feeling that
it's gone too soon.
The canvas of the sky painted with an abundance of
color.
So I wait here on my stone until nature crates
another

## Before I Drowned

I emptied out my mind today of thoughts of
yesteryear
I put them all on lined pages that I hold oh so dear
I lock the book away in a location only I can find
But wouldn't you do the same if you had a book that
exposed your mind
I could never allow anyone to read even a page of
my thoughts
For then they would know to much and ridicule me
for my faults
I know I'm not perfect and believe me I don't try to
be either
But you see I use this fake image of me 24-7 and at
times I need a breather
I just don't know that if you knew that real me, the
me that I defend,
That you couldn't look me in my eye and claim me
as a friend
Its not a chance I'm willing to take not at this point

in my life

I've seen too many come and go and dealt with to

much strife

I emptied out my mind today of thoughts that I have

kept

And flushed them out before I drowned in its depth

## Blind Eye
### *Acrostic*

Bound by natures will

Loved by the daughters of the Gods

In tuned to sounds echoes

Nurturing his audio eyes

Driven by a more beautiful sight


Much to humble to be belittled

Anchored to mans true self

No dark place looks the

Same, yet he knows nothing


Else, closed eyes can visit

Young minds ask most

Everyone wonders

Sick eyes see most

# Clay-Maker

Young moldable mind
Putty of clay spinning about
The turn table woven within
The fingers of the father
Folded and carved in only
The manner he desired

It hurt many times
The scarring that was suffered
Like freshly split skin from
A ragged, worn back
Still forces to remain immune
To the constant punishment

Skin would pull tightly
At just the sound of arrival
Heart beating much to fast to be
Held in place by simple Bones.
Fear is now
Taking shape still no
Illustration is capable to be
Displayed to strangers

15

That was not an ability he
Instilled in his creation
Tears were never revealed
To the creator instead hid and held
Tightly inside a flask

Bright days made darker
Nights black and still
Cold shivering muscles
Unable to calm oneself

Keep it all bottled inside
No tip no sound no hint
All kept inside this is how
A man is made so the
Creator said
This is how a boys
Young beautiful mind
Is corrupted says me

## Dear Santa

Dear Santa,

It's just me, ten year old Timothy. I know I've written you before but if you could do me this favor my last letter you can ignore. I know I asked for toys this year, a bike and a race car set, some army men a baseball glove and a remote control corvette. I haven't been the best behaved, this year just wasn't my best, but they say you see everything so I'm sure you saw my test. I'll admit to you the faults I've made the stealing and the smoking; you see you're my last resort prior to my family being completely broken. My dialog just isn't working and bruises are my consolation prize. So despite this past year's pitfalls, will you wipe this child's eyes? All I want for Christmas this year will take up little room on your pad, if you have time on your trip around the globe please help MOM and DAD

## Do You Hate Me

Do you hate me cause you aint me
Cause your smile don't light up a dark place
Do you put me down because your eyes can't
escape my face?
Do you hate me because my skin is the color of coal
from the ground your God created?
Or because yours will become as mine after natural
or cremated
Do you hate me because I smile after you shoot me
down with words?
Do you dislike me cause I'm open minded knowing
n-i-g-g-e-r is just a word
Does it offend you that I don't offend you?
And my mood is as warm as the day is bright
Do you hate me because deep down you know your
wrong and I'm right?

## Do You Know What Love Means

*If only they could see me and not my exterior complexity. Even while their eyes may remain open to sight they seem blinded by a darker veil. I seem to be one of the few that can do what I can. If only everyone could see with the sight of a thousands eyes, listen with their hearts and not their ears, Feel with their souls instead of their hands and help with their full essence and not their mouths. We all use the word love as if it always applies being completely shielded from our own souls. If you knew what goes on inside my inner shell no love would be mine. As to you, would love be yours? My caves remain undiscovered my caverns unconquered and no bright love can linger where Darkness rules as king. So how can you say you love? Only when you crossed my deserts and swam my ocean as I do everyday can you reach me. Then we'll travel over my mountains and explore my caves, fight my demons and chase my heart. They use the word love as if they mean it smiling behind blank stares and empty conversation. I'll care not for your body nor your eyes or stare I'm in search of only your soul...*

19

*THAT'S MY LOVE TO YOU!*

## Don't Forget to Pass it On

Don't forget to pass it on as the sun sets on his life
and rises on my dawn
But my fate has been decided, I was there for the
decision
They care very little for his excuses that he was
raised with no supervision
His personality means nothing it played no role in
their acts
They cared very little about what he did with his life
as he addressed them with the facts
I guess it's not what he did or didn't do that
condemned him to hell
It was his own self heart that embodies him in his
cell
I was there throughout my own trail although on the
defense I was not
And although I wasn't being persecuted, morally I
was on the spot
I was there for my own conviction I stared into
judgments eye
I was there for my own execution and I know where
the souls of the damned lie

I didn't feel the pain of death because I wasn't the

one being hurt

But I could still hear the agonizing screams as I

buried the ones who could in the dirt

And so my fate has been decided and now you're

here for my end

But beware you could face a similar situation for us

all share the same sin

And now you can see your won trial although you'll

be the one they try to convince

And you will see your own conviction although I'll

be the one behind deaths fence

And you will see your own execution

Although I'll be the one screaming

And the images of me will remain with you even

while you attempt dreaming

Now as the sun set on my life for now yours has just

dawned

So take the knowledge I've expressed and don't

forget to pass it on

## Dreams

My dreams are as clouds in the sky
Both enormous and so easy to come by
They float as clouds do inside my own blue lagoon
They break apart and piece together as does the
great silver moon
My dreams are like your stars that glow during your
twilight lumber
And I hold them all so close, you see to each I give
a number
I could tell you each one in extraordinary detail
believe me I can
Some as huge as the majestic mountains some as
small as a grain of sand
My dreams grow as high as your great tree tops,
swaying in the breeze of my brainstorm
To venture to deeply inside varies greatly from
society's norm
In my dreams is where my reality truly lives
And I could live for centuries on the sustenance it
gives
My dreams are as clouds in the sky
So, quickly off to sleep I close my eyes.

## Dust to Dust

Soldiers to dust turned

Swayed by winds gentle movements

Ashes to Ashes

## Fall is Here

The sun is orange just behind those hills and I
wonder if I could ever go there. Its right beyond that
mountains slope and I believe that I could reach it.
Even if I could would it still be as beautiful or
would it lose a portion of it radiance. The leaves are
turning orange red and yellow and I ponder about
their descent. Are they frightened at all by the fall
or are they deceased. Do they even feel pain do they
know what's happening to them. Or maybe it's the
tree that loses a dear friend. Or has she grown
accustomed to her children leaving time after time.
The air is slightly bitter then the other seasons as I
taste the fresh rain. The sky is filled with pictures
yet I am ignorant to what they are it's as if God had
drawn it himself every-year waiting for this moment
to impress us all…
FALL IS HERE AGAIN

## First Day of Winter

Cold winters dew frost

Tickles children's playful hearts

Glazing fields abroad

## First night

*He was devoted to her*
*Pureness, her untouched self*
*Her solidarity of sexuality*
*As untamed as a fresh fallen*
*Snow amidst the forest floor*

*After their prenuptial*
*Her pearl white*
*Dress would melt away*
*Unleashing her sexual*
*Desire, craving the touch*
*Of her man*

*Scores of hormones*
*Continually lap her brain*
*Her fluids fill her vulva*
*Swollen tight with love*

*He runs his fingers through*
*Her hair lying her down*
*Upon the cloud,*
*Miles away from*
*Prying eyes*

*Where only the two*
*Exist to satisfy*
*And extinguish their*
*Own passionate fire*

*She places her soul*
*Atop of his body*
*Granting his traveler*
*Entry through-out*
*Her milky valley*

*Intercourse of Ecstasy*
*Was only the first*
*Interpretation of his love*
*He yearned to taste her*
*Rivers and bathe in*
*Her lakes*

*After dancing in the*
*Halls of orgasmic*
*Pleasure she lead him*
*To the home of*
*Fluid streams*

*Tongue pressed against*
*Her womanhood, muscle*
*Control lost for all*
*Extremities, caution*
*Thrown to the wind*

*She now knows what it means*
*To save herself*
*She is now mine*
*She is now a woman*

## Help her

She told me that she would not last

In a house which forced walking on broken glass

In which shadowy figures haunt her dreams

And the hallway to her room it seems

The markings on her flesh were proof

Of clear mistreatment in her youth

She told me her screams went unheeded

And the help never came that she needed

She pushed aside her tears of pain

As her father pushed her again and again

The stripes she wore were not her own

And even while at home she was never home

So who is going to assist the poor little girl?

Who is going to protect her world

She said she had no shoulder on which to cry

So she feels her only option is to die

Who will come to her aid?

To shield and protect from the shade

Before she does what her mind demands

And takes her life with her own hand

## Her and Him

He always made her smile
He sometimes made her cry
He never made her happy
Yet she never asked why

He always brought her flowers
He sometimes held her hand
He never mentioned infidelity
When he departed to foreign lands

She always asked the questions
She sometimes believed his lies
She never stopped loving him
A vow she took to die

She always wanted more
She sometimes wanted less
She never wanted a broken heart
But he deals those the best

## I Don't Know What I Don't Know

If your heart is broken yet you manage a smile
I don't know what you don't show
When your beaches are sandy yet you lack the tides
of others
I don't know when your lights are dimmed to a glow
No matter the fury that ones oceans exhale
On winds in which to fatten their sails
I don't know what I don't know

## I Don't Want to Love You

*Don't ask me to love you*
*Don't ask me to cross the sea of wonder and joy*
*And take part in the relationship that entraps both*
*girl and boy*
*Don't ask me to take part in your heart*
*Or to swim in your soul*
*To be the half that makes you whole*
*Don't make me say I love you*
*Don't make me worship the ground you walk on*
*And bless the clouds above you*
*Don't request my heart to skip a beat*
*Or feel the magnetism from across the street*
*Don't invade my thoughts with you presence*
*And detour all else aside*
*Don't make me miss your essence*
*My heart to seek yours to hide*
*Don't make me want to call your name*
*Just to force what's left of me insane*
*Please don't ask me to endure this sin*
*And make me love you once again*

## I Don't Want to Stay

Maybe I don't want to stay here, if I did what would be my reason? Even as I walk down the street I watch people decompose into their own self nothingness. There is no need for me to remain, I feel no obligation to this place. Besides I was given to the world it was in no way bestowed to me. I feel as though I am property of society and in no way am I my own. I have no say in my fate continuing here. Maybe I don't want to stay I'll leave by wind upon the dreams of night; my figure will cast no more shadows upon this misused ground and step no limb throughout the soil. No more shall I breathe in my own recoil of life. I will no longer be a tangible part of this realm and my own imagery will deplete. I don't want to stay.............What love am I to be, who am I to confide in, or in me, who is to smile upon my face and take my extension of hope. Who will take hold of my hand and shield me.

## I Met Him Today

He introduced himself to me for the first time his

name the same as mine.

"What a coincidence"

He told me many of his hobbies as I expressed my

own and found they were strikingly similar

"What a coincidence"

His dreams and aspirations all parallel to my own

"What a coincidence"

Then he showed his darker side death suffering

heartache, and guilt, he said he had thoughts of

murder and rituals of another world

All I could say was

"What a coincidence"

# I Wish

I wish I could be as you smiling at what life deals
So carefree in your decisions it's such an unfamiliar
feel
It's like uncharted territory, an expedition on which
I've never been
I won't even know where to begin so often I'd
pretend
I wish I could be like him, his life seem full of joy
He seems to have it under control, I wish I was that
boy
I wish I could be as you, your life has a meaningful
twirl
There is no heartache for what's to come
I wish I was that girl
I wish I could be as you, and see the world as a
grain of sand
And always be in high sprits I wish I was that man
I wish I was you and never had dreams of the end
If only I could be as strong as that I wish I was that
woman

I wish I could be as you and saw life so mellow and
mild
To be cared upon day and night I wish I was that
child
I wish I could be any of you it appears so easy to be
But perhaps you're staring at my exterior and
wishing you were me

# I'll Say It

*Can you hear what I'm saying to you these words I know I've never used before? The enchanted whisper of a once silenced heart. Yet the meaning is true in depths as deep as the core. Listen closely and see if you can hear the mumbling sound. It's distinctive to your own yet still so profound. Can you see what I'm saying to you can't you see the weakness in my knee. Observe the quiver in my lip the unsteadiness of me. I can't speak, move, or even breathe when you are around. I'm afraid I'll move the wrong way, say the wrong thing, or miss your voice sweet sound. Can you feel what I'm saying to you as my pulse races my heart beats faster? And this is the only way I can express these thoughts. Praying that it won't be a disaster my lips form to say the words. The words that describe the acts I do I await my time and at the right moment I'll say*

*I LOVE YOU*

## Inspiration

Listen, listen to the words, what do they say to you
what are they trying to convey? Are they
whispering sweetly or starving for the attention of
the reader. Listen to everything conversations, the
lines they use in movies, the saying you read on
bumper sticker listen to them all

Watch, watch it all, every tree that blows in the
majesty of the wind, each cloud that crosses your
path, then write about how it changed your life, and
it always does; every gust, every sight, in some way
reacts to the rest of our outlook, watch it all.

Feel, feel it all, the warmth of the new day, the
spray of the oceans tide as you stand on the shores
that only you own. Feel how amazing it is to take
that deep breath, to sustain the life you were granted

Express, express the sounds your very own way.
See the world the way that makes you smile on a
gloomy day. See it the way that we were meant to
see it, express the feeling of love, of warmth, and
yourself.

### .Johnny Brown

In a darkened room
Johnny Brown stands

The object
Of a multitudes obsession

A single bead of sweat
Relinquishes its hold on his
Brow and smacks the wood surface

Anticipation bellows in
His stomach watching
The pearls of eyes
Studying his own

Soft melody reminisce
Of a young Louie Armstrong

Soothing the mass with
The sweet feel of
Love in the air

Silky red glow
Made its way
Out of his saxophone
And across every guys
Pretty girl's face.

Toes tap in unison
Shoulders sway in
The sounds breeze
Fingers snap lightly
Ambient sound

Ivory bars replaced
With magical waves
Entrancing the mind
Hypnotizing its subjects

Lovers glide to their
Feet and step onto
Clouds about the wind

Quarrels buried far
And who cares where
You dance on this song of air

**Now that's Jazz Johnny!**

## Just a Lil Weed

Man, don't you know it takes me there
With all I worry about
One hit and I don't have to care

If I could I'd leave my head in the clouds
Stay high forever
Believe me no doubt

I need to take two hits
Just to take two hits
After that it's warfare
Against potato chips

I can focus, drive and smoke some more
While riding Mary Jane
Lounging up on cloud four

Just a hop from sexy ol'
Cloud nine, And I'm headed there next
To get me mine

Because after I smoke
I'm hard as a Missile
And with impaired vision
Any women's official

I just don't get what all the fuss is about
Mr. Bush you want to see real archery
Let there be a weed drought

Just pass the bong, pipe, or blunt
After this we'll smoke again
I got all you want

## Just Outside My Window

The wars of my father's father,
Kills in my sons battlefields
Imagine that four generations of
Tribulations. No angelic words
Spoken for these men's ears
To hear

The slaves of a puppet master
Famine abuse hid from the masses
Covered with a simpletons fancy, wide eyed
Mouth agape, at strangers mind
Corrupting misdeeds

Infestations linger in the wombs
Of our brothers and sisters. Fallen to the
Dusty earth. The scent of our ancestors
Brought by way of the wind.
Turned blind eye and simply an illusion.

Death stands on many of our own
Street corners feeding the disease
The walking dead passes for the
Living all the while their blood
Poisoned, chased down by the
Wolves of the effects
Sooner or later.

Global phenomenon toys with
Society's way of life, still some
Graze about our fertile mothers
Essence blindly following
Those we don't know into extinction
And it's all just outside my window.

## Knocking on Heaven's Door

The day St.Gabriel

Blows his horn

And the fallen

Arise from their

Graves.

When the ears of

Saved will ring

In recognition

Every nation one

In the same

When the sun

Shines so bright

The moon is no

Longer known to

Mankind and the eyes of

The demons melt away

No shadows to cast

Or caverns to explore

Every soul stood at

Attention

Sinners called from
Their caves to
Be held for their
Ways, the wicked close
To follow.

And one by one
Were held accountable
Each sin spelled
Word for word

Some granted entry
Others only teased
At the idea, prior
To facing their fate

When it is me who
Stands before
Peter at the gates
Of eternity fist
Clenched of past
Wrongdoings

And St.Gabriel ask me of

My heart; Have

I loved enough,

Have I let love and

If I used the gifts

Given


Have I sinned

To much, made others

Sin, or stood blind

To obvious wrong doings


With no one else

For me to cast blame

No friends or family

By my side


Angel eyes witness

My doubt, no words

Or muscles to move


All I can do is

Plead ....Please

## Last Night

Last night I dreamt a dream indeed

As I lay in my bed at ease

I dreamt I was upon eagles wings

And soared across the breeze

It begun in my lands of course, land so familiar to

me

Then we flew to a country side flooded with sin and

poverty

The eagle showed me armies of the past and

revolutions yet to come

Of kings betrayed and nations slain the slander that

was done

form distant land to far off place, from shore to

shore we glide

Disease, famine, raid, and riot the eagle uncovered

each lie

He showed me truths unknown to my mind and

visions unseen to my soul

We visited the searing sands of my forefathers and

experienced the mountains peaks cold

From there I could see the tears of souls as far as

earths opposite peak

They show no mercy, those in power whose name I

CARE not speak

I board the mighty bird again

And fly directly to the Vatican

To speak for a moment to the pope

For if nothing else a glimmer of hope

For a land as a whole I doubt can make it

And a people in pain refusing to take it

I awoke the next morning as any other man

Only with memories of bitter cold and burning sand

Of dynasties fallen and treacheries rise

And mothers with lost sons and tears in their eyes

Last night I dreamt a dream indeed

That not just mine but all people are in need

## Leaves

Scattered leaves paint earth

Bending to winds mere motion

God's paintbrush of art

## Life Cycle

Springs sun brings earths fruit

Seedlings sprout to reach the sun

Spread then seed their own

## Little Boy Blue

If you have never heard the story of little boy blue
Please take a seat and I shall explain it to you
You see little boy blue had a name at one point and
time
But through the days, weeks, months, and years it
has seemed to slip our minds
You see not many cared about little boy blue; not
because of anything that he had done
He had never known a normal life of playing and
having fun
Little boy blue lead a different life although many
may not comprehend
But he would try to mimic the lives of others; he
said he could always pretend
Little boy blue what happen to you, you fell down
the steps today?
And the bruises on your arm the steps did the harm
are you sure that your ok
He smile and nodded he'd be ok and whispered he
had played dangerously that day
I smiled back and said please be careful from this
point on

He looked at me face full of glee and said his word was sworn

Little boy blue what happen to you how did you get that burn?

He looked at me frightfully and said it was none of my concern

Perhaps he needed space so I didn't say another word

And when he described a picture he drew he wished to be as free as a bird

Little boy blue what ever do you mean please explain to me

He left the room as depressed as he had come uttering just let me be

Little boy blue what happen to you why are you all covered up?

And what is that? Wait come closer, on your face is that make-up?

Little boy blue who did this to you, you can tell me I'm your friend

He looked at me and said leave me alone all I want is to pretend

Little boy blue what happen to you haven't seen you in so long

You have not come by to see me I hope there is
nothing wrong
Little boy blue what happen to you last night you
were in dreams
And even when I awoke in my head I could still
hear your screams
Little boy blue what happen to you I finally heard
when you cried
But I was much too late for little boy blue you see
he had already died
So that's the story of little boy blue and I've only left
out one fact
In my dream he said he never told me because he
wanted to make an impact
I've had this dream time and time again and he used
this as his excuse
And said I am to write it down to help stop child
abuse.

## Loss One

She told me that she had to go
And leave she did that very night
All I could do was watch as my heart walked
Through the door and what was I to do but watch

Watch as my life changes
Right in front of my eyes
Watch as five years of memories
Began to become just a distant
Thought a glimmer of light
In the starry sky that is my guide

That's all she left me with
These images these fragments of thought
These mental sounds that echo
Through my skulls empty
Caverns

Before I could say stay she
Was gone, my blue birds
Song she's heard before so used
To my melody simply immune to
My tune of love

So it's just me in my own nothingness
She told me that she
Had to go and go she did

## Maybe

Maybe I don't want to stay here if I did what would
be the reason? Even as I walk down the street I
watch people decompose into their own self
nothingness. There is no need for me to remain I
have no obligation to this place, besides I was given
to this world it was not given to me. I feel as though
I am property and in no way am I my own, I have
no say in my own fate continuing here.
Maybe I don't want to stay…
I'll leave by wind upon the dream of night. I'll cast
no more shadows upon this ground and step no limb
throughout this soil. No more shall I breathe in my
very own recoil of life I will no longer be tangible
and my own imagery depletes.
Maybe I don't want to stay…
What love am I to be, who am I to confide in or
who in me? Who is to smile upon my face and take
my extension of self?

## Messages From a Lover

There once was a man named......well we wont
name him until his deed is done.
Either lose his soul or valor be won.
To love was, he would say, his true calling.
Much too soft of a heart so it kept the man falling.
Ever so deeply into loves abyss.
To absolutely no end, no hit or miss
The object of affection his wife of many years.
Those happy moments nothing but a whisper in his
ears.
There were flowers, candy, and cards he would
write.
He'd give her poetry for her mind and paintings for
sight.
He'd not give her up for all earthly treasure.
Not soil nor sky or mighty control of the weather.
This man he loved deeply, too deeply some would
say.
Such blindness in love can lead to betray.
It crept in his thoughts of his love being untrue.
Of nights without her and days of past scent.

*Which left memories of happiness both mangled and*
*bent.*
*His love had gone and adjoined with another.*
*So he found himself an empty shell of a lover.*
*With his love turned sour its sweet fruit made bitter.*
*His mind felt little remorse with parting with her.*
*So He found himself at fates crossroad.*
*To take two lives and let their blood run cold.*
*Or take no lives, could he be so bold.*
*The left road he chose in which to deal.*
*You see love had forced him to kill.*
*So what would you name him a killer or lover.*
*Is it such a crime to love so much toward another?*

## My Addict

It calls out to him, yelling his name

Pleading for the sensation the rush in the veins

The excitement of the night

The flashing of the lights

His body thinks he needs it yet his brain can hardly

cope

He battles within himself silently screaming for

hope

It calls so much louder then any other voice he can

hear

And it's fueled by his self loathing and kept burning

by the fires of fear

He yearns for the burn, the trip, the ride

He's blinded by the impulses, rationality pushed

aside

He has been down this road five times just today

He's poisoned himself in a mutilating way

He's open the door for his mixture to invade

No walls to block no helpful aid

He feels he deserves this kind of pain

And fishes aimlessly for his next vein

To no other substance would he summit

This is volume 1 of my addict

# My Addict (part 2)

It takes her to another place where caring isn't the

norm

She uses it as her life raft to carry her through the

storm

She claims it doesn't interfere, it calms and sooths

her mind

But outsides looking in feel she's reincarnated into a

different kind

She has chosen it over her own seed

Her flesh, her blood yet only the addition she'll feed

Eyes clouded and grey

Pitch black pupils

Completely disoriented, a mere zombie of the day

It's devoured the mind consumed the soul

Materialized in reality, black as coal

It plays the motor skills in ways totally erratic

This is her story; part 2 of my addict

# My Letter

I've told this paper endless thoughts

My minds interior and physical faults

Of dreams and nightmares scarring my mind

Leaving me limp and paralyzed in the fields behind

I've express to it the rage of me

And was left with unknowing uncertainty

If it could keep my shadows hidden

And show no one, for I have signed them forbidden

Not even my eyes I want it to show

So why tell the paper, that *I DON'T KNOW*

I've bled my emotions on every line

Believe me in truth I've opened up my mind

I've told this paper so much of me

I've given it the power to completely judge me

I've unarmed my guards and told them to leave the
door

And decided that I will hide no more

So I've sent this paper off to you

In response to me finally being true

Within this letter lay the context of my soul

Not part, or half, this time it's whole

# My Little Girl

I'll tell you about my smile, my smile stands two

feet high

And if push came to shove for my smile I'd die

My smile gives me a reason to live

And a direction for my heart to give

My smile can brighten any dampened mood

And for any starving drought it will be my food


I'll tell you about my love, my love calls out to me

And doesn't scorn me for being me

My love runs across the room and into these arms of

mine

It's forced me to realize how little time

There really is for me to love

But when I go I'll watch from above


I'll tell you about my joy, my joy calls me dad

And I couldn't imagine the life I could have had

Without hearing that angelic voice

My joy gives me the choice

And I choose to be her best friend

Throughout bitter cold and blowing wind

She is why I smile

She is why I love

She is my joy

She is my world

She is my little baby girl

## No One Knows

No one knows why I cry maybe it's because I never
tell

Perhaps it's because I only do it when I'm alone

And they weren't present when each tear fell

I don't know why I've regressed and went into my
own

And no one asked any questions when I darkened
my entire home

No one knows why communication I've cut off to
all souls

And any type of expectations have diminished with
my goals

No one noticed the downward spiral as it begun

And no one noticed that I only come out when the
sky goes to sleep with the sun

No ones knows why I'm not there where I have
previously been

And none seem to notice the ghostly marks as they
appear on my skin

No one knows my mysteries, it's a place no man
dares

No one noticed I'm no longer a part of this place I
guess no on cares

## On a Whim

Don't tell me what I want to hear
Tell me what I need to know
Don't tell me I'm a shinning light
Show me how I glow
Don't pity me in times of stress
I'm working through my tribulations
Don't be so quick to rush to my aid
Please use hesitation
Don't try to describe the voice of angels
Give me ears to hear the song
And don't exclude me from the love they show
Give me script to sing along

## Place Unknown

There is no escape from this place that's not on a
map yet we all have been there
It's an unorthodox paradise for those who don't care
If you listen, truly listen you'll hear sobs carried by
the wind
Pleas for help, a hand, or a shoulder on which to
lean
Despite its high population seldom is another soul
seen.
I've journeyed to this place more then I'd care to
admit
I've been beaten and scared and the world just
wasn't worth it
So I left it all behind walked through the jungles of
isolation
Swam the seas of my own cruel imagination
Until I reached the shores of this place
Where hearing sobs and seeing no face
Is an experience that is all to familiar to me

COME FURTHER IF YOU WANT TO SEE.......



This place I'll lead you is called Alone

Where sorrow lives and souls groan

Where pity is nowhere and heartache is the air we

breathe

Where it's easy to find yourself trapped and

seemingly impossible to leave

WELCOME TO ALONE!

## Planes, Trains, and Automobiles

My love I'm on my way to you from Paris I took a
plane

Then abroad the 1:15 in Jamestown and a short nap
on the train

Knowing the seconds are melting away is the only
way I deal

Then directly to your arms by way of automobile

## Rejoice

Through black widows gate
doth pass all God's lost children
Saved by Noah's doves

## Sailor's Souls

Dark seas mirror moon

Revealing souls lost in blue

Trapped in endless night

## Same Old Joke

I've fallen for it again
Fallen for the same old joke
It's never told any
Differently just new faces telling
Me the same joke

You would think one
Would grow weary of
The same setup
The same punch line
But it gets me every time

I just can't help but
Indulge in a fair faced
Beauty seductive humors
So I clutch my sides
And hand over my heart

I've fallen in love
With my new comedian
Just as I have with
The past funny women
That fate as intertwined
My path with

I've fallen in love
With the idea of
Someone loving one
Of the fallen
But all I learned
Was what a
Joke Love Is.

## Save Room

Save some room for me
When you jot down in your book

Reminisce lovingly
When you give your past a look

Remember anniversaries, birthdays
And in those special moments

The love we made the getaways
The good morning darling sonnets

Don't allow your memory to exclude
The vast mountain of roses

But brush right over my attitude
And the times it got ferocious

Remember the times that we held hands
Or talked on the phone for hours

The moon lit walks we took on the sands
Or danced in the warming morning showers

So when you're writing down
All your life's forget-me-nots

I hope this reminds you of my sound
And you save for me, at least a spot

## Secret of Life

The secret of life is complex in many ways
It tends to become even more so as we approach the
end of our days
You see as we grow older we forget the truth
As hard as it is to believe we had the answers in our
youth
Through the years we forget the facts that we were
told
It slipped our minds as we began to grow old
The answer lies in each infant that is born into this
world
Each bundle of wonder each boy and girl
So go, go ask the child why its first instinct is to cry
It's because they know the secrets of life
That in the end we all die.

## Smile

I don't smile because I'm happy and it's not because
I'm sad
I don't smile because of a joke of loves that I've had
It's not just so you can see the grin upon my face
I don't smile because of the joy, and freedom of
open space
I don't smile because I have to whenever you come
around
I don't smile because of the sky or because of the
ground
Neither Heaven nor hell put this smile on my face
I could smile anywhere and any kind of place

## Sometimes

Sometimes I want to cry & there seems to be no

reason at all

Sometimes I want to jump but I am afraid of the fall

Sometimes I want to scream so everyone knows my

thought

Sometimes I want to blame but it seems to be my

fault

Sometimes I want to change but I return to where I

begun

And sometimes it seems when I reach for the sky I

get burned by the sun

Sometimes I want to expand but my mind entraps

its own creations

Sometimes I want to say goodbye and all I get are

salutations

There are times I feel left out when in fact I am the

main attraction

Then there are times I do the unexpected and still

get no reaction

Sometimes I want to be left alone yet the crowd

seems to come to me

Then there are times when I search for a soul and

find myself lost at sea

Sometimes I feel loved when in fact its abuse

Then there are times I have inner battles and all I

want is a truce

Sometimes I'll brainstorm when I wish for calmer

tide

Then there are nights I want to sleep yet my body

won't abide

Sometimes I need to be pinched to be sure I'm still

alive

But no matter what I'll express myself and in that

I'll survive.

## Sometimes (part 2)

Sometimes I want to cry but the tears wont help my
pain
And sometimes I want the sun and instead I get rain
Sometimes I want to breathe but my lungs won't
hold the air
Sometimes I want to tell a soul but I can't find one
who cares
Sometimes I'm looking for the sea when instead I
get a pond or lake
Sometimes I want to right my wrongs but I have too
many mistakes
Sometimes I want to escape the darkness but the
night seems endless to me
Sometimes I want to be left alone but my dreams
won't let me be
Sometimes all I want is to dream when only
nightmares invade my mind
And sometimes it's hard to see the light because I'm
blinded by the shine

Sometimes I wait for the sun to raise yet mine sets
and there's gloom
Sometimes I await my rebirth but I'm constantly
interrupted by my own doom

## Sometimes (part3)

Sometimes time, it just stands still no matter the

case I am unable to reach the hill

Sometimes my heart drops and I am completely

unable to deal

Sometimes I gaze at the stars and ponder there

conversation

Sometimes the beauty of her eyes create their own

constellation

Sometimes I'm completely silent yet they know

what I want to say

Sometimes I can see exactly what's wrong with this

world though I'm stuck in yesterday

Sometimes I fell I could lose control and go out of

my mind

Sometimes I go through it all, but now .......now is

not one of those times

## Sometimes (part 4)

Sometimes I need a helping hand

When instead I get the cold shoulder

And sometimes I need the courage of a man

Despite that, I get passed over

Sometimes only the stormy night

Is my one solitude

And sometimes my minds so full of fright

I'm unable to stabilize the mood

Sometimes my simple pride

Can take advantage and over ride

The rationale my love ones speak

To my empty heart that constantly leaks

And sometimes I can control myself

And place my demons on the shelf

Sometimes they'll obey my desires

And release me from my own hell fires

Sometimes I can escape my prison

Temporarily my soul then risen

But this entrapment is my curse to bear

It's branded in my depth

I've never asked for one to care

This curse for me I've kept

Sometimes I don't know who I am

So I question all I see

Much too often I'm lost in the abyss

And I can't even trust me

Sometimes I try to escape my shadows

But there much more clever then I could have

imagined

And sometimes love is an emotion that I can't afford

But more often then that its compassion

## Sorrow

Sorrow

Despair, heartache

Tears roll slowly

Loss, abandonment and sadness

State of mind

## Summer's Gift

Shimmering Valleys
Drenched in the burning sun rays
Brings fourth summers love

## The Day My Muse Walked Out

The day my muse walked out was
Not unlike any other
We had put beyond our reach,
Same father sky warming
His better half mother earth

The deja vu of her stubbornness
Assured me of a frozen
Pipeline through which
Inspiration traveled

The magic factory where
Words, themes, and titles
Were conjured completely
Vanished, though I knew
This is where she kept them

No longer did I share
Her ears that allowed
Me to listen between the
Words of a false man's
Speech or a lame creature's sorrows

As unorthodox as my pen
To pad was my rhythm to
Reason, feelings made
Indescribable she left
My heart unresponsive

Binding my writing arm
Behind my back, forcing
Me to adapt. Knowing my
Own fortitude she maliciously
Stole my other rendering me
Creatively hopeless

She torments me with
Glimpses of her sorcery
Only to remind me of
My own pitiful state of
Mind without her grace.

I'm her puppet without strings
Limp mangled on the canvas
Of a balled up piece of notebook Paper,
my 33rd attempt at poetic enlightenment

Many times I feared she
Would implant her witchcraft
Into another souls mind.
Leaving me as emotionally
Dead as so many of the rest

She made the tears dry before
They left my eyes,
Striping what's left of any
Kind of discharge that could
Show my clear downheartedness

Now I can only pray
When I'm reincarnated
I'm blessed with another
Enlightened muse such as she

The day my muse walked out
Was not unlike any other
Day, other then it was then
I knew I could not live without her.

## The Entryway

Standing at the entryway…

Waiting for the next calm
To tame the Vodka storm,
My wondering mind

Lost in an alcoholic
Forest bound by
Tress of bourbon and scotch,
Dripping their sweat

Onto my head
Soaking through my
Cranium feeding
Ideas and thoughts to
My cerebral cortex

Standing at the entryway…

Peach schnapps
Nourishes the great
Rivers and lakes I

Respectfully call my
Adversaries.

Gin permeates the clouds
Only to release the
Tensions onto this
Forest dwellers liver

The fog of inebriation
Rules with an iron
Fist just beyond the
Heineken Falls

Standing at the entryway

This is where my
Eyes are glazed
And visions often
Double team me,
Cornering me

My legs mere strings
Much to feeble
To gain the advantage

Over the flattest of soil

Cirrhosis was born
As my true nemesis
Tracking me down
As its prey

Scraping away in
My miserable attempt
To escape my predators
Clutches, I decide to
Walk through the entryway

"Hello Welcome to A.A"

# The Planter's Field

I'm terrified of the planter's field; no substance
from it is ripe
We only build the courage once to journey to the
farm of black misty night
The farmer himself I've never seen and he has no
lack of seeds to plant
In many ways he's a magic worker last wishes he
would grant
His process never changes true he's stubborn to the
bone
First dig then seed, cover it up, on top he'd place a
stone
His shadowy figure rules his farm as a king rules his
land
No seed he plant shall ever bare fruit no matter the
loved ones demands
I'm so afraid of the planter's field no life there ever
remains
And every seed that he encounters that body he now
claims

I'll never travel to the planter's field I'm afraid of
what's to pass
But I know that when I do arrive that journey will
be my last.

## This World

Perhaps this world is another's very pit of damnation. If so many questions would be answered then never again would I be surprised by the horrible actions of the beings left here to suffer. I would never again dream of a malnourished land, mothers with their dying children in hand, without a tear to shed, forced to accept this inevitable pain that blows in the wind and fills theirs lungs. Maybe this is the place all the holy books speak of when they refer to the uncontrollable abyss. When all I can see are man made structures being fueled by disease stricken masses. Maybe this is the home of torment that the elders spoke of. What have I done to deserve the sights of homelessness and murder, rape and abandonment, that reside in this world we were given. This can't be it, this can't be the place where I am to raise my children, next to the dying infants screaming for a liberator. I refuse to build my home on top of the ravaged ruins of my fellow mans hopes. Yet these are the options we were given but not in your home, not within the walls that protect and hold your family, not there does death and mistreatment live so why bother.

## Touch

*She tried to satisfy*
*His cravings, all attempts*
*Fell short of their goal*
*She soaked his skin in*
*Lotions, bathed in*
*Sensual oils all*
*To no avail*

*Floated her body*
*Across his influence,*
*Stroked and rubbed his pride*
*Gently massaged his ego*
*Still unable to light the fire*
*To his lust*

*She meets another form*
*Identical to her own.*
*Floodgates unable to*
*Contain her estrogen*
*Heart open needing the*
*Touch*

*The passion widow*
*Broke sexual grounds*
*Soft lips pressed tightly*
*Outer slips fall to the*
*Floor the smell of*
*One another's perfume*
*Resonates throughout*
*The sheets*

*The delicate brush*
*Of a woman was like*
*The freshness of a ripe*
*Peach's oozing juices*
*Over her lip gloss*
*She embraced the*
*Experience*

*Her tongue was her*
*Newest appendage sliding*
*About the feminine cave*
*Searching for place*
*Where pleasure lives*
*The place where her*
*Partner held the*
*Pit of her peach*

*Taste the sweetest*
*Fruit, moisten the*
*Scared seed orgasms*
*Erupting love is made*

# TREATMENT

My symptoms you ask?

Chronic depression
And an uncontrollable obsession
I well up at the sight
Of a normal mans delight
I can take no pleasure
In everyday measures
My heart is much to dark
For any light of yours to spark
I'm lost out at sea
And just left to be

His diagnosis…

I want you to talk to my friend
He has dealt with problems within
He'll prescribe perhaps a pill
Which will make it easier to deal
He'll talk to you a while
Digging deeper until you smile
He'll bring out that inner glow

Trust me I know
You come back in say a week
You'll sit; you and I will speak

The results

The week has passed I'm here to tell
I'm still locked in my emotional cell
My symptoms have remained to be
Stuck seemingly inside of me
And more I gain everyday
Sadness, heartache, with nothing to say
The feelings have crossed into the physical plane
My joints they ache my skin is plain

His final assessment

I've done for you all I can
And I just may understand
My past diagnoses it was wrong
Its good we met again before to long
I'll send you to another friend of mine
With her you should spend more time

## My conclusion

I've wrestled with these demons here
I've talked to strangers and exposed my fear
I've heard every word they have had to say
And still I sit here despondent this way
I've found my cure to all this strife
There is no cure for life

# Unknown

It's dark all around me even when I open my eyes
wide
There are noises in every direction and I feel
something by my side
These voices many of which I have never heard
They seem to know me intimately although it may
sound absurd
They speak to me and tell me to perform unsightly
actions
I can't concentrate on the simple things in life my
mind is its own distraction
I need to get out but as you know there is no escape
from yourself
No escape from what's inside no escape from
what's being dealt
I'm being held and bound by my own imagery
And a slave to my own imagination

## Where I'll Be

You can find me
On the purple hill
Behind the bush that
Grew too tall

Or playing connect
The dots with stars
Or marbles with the
Ones that fall

Soaring on the backs
Of unicorns or chasing
Down forest gnomes

Or perhaps atop
A rainbow
The place that I call home

You can find me where
Up is down with underwater
Walkers unable to drown

Where night is bright
Like daytime light
And sugar treats
Are the biggest fright

If you want to find
Me there I'll be
In the only place
I can be me

My very own Insanity

## Who needs it?

Who needs love who needs to be hurt day in and
day out?
Who needs the affection, when the other person
decides to drop out?
Who needs companionship when it often ends in a
struggle?
Who needs the commitment to marriage when the
break-up hurts double?
Who need protection when your plan is to release
me into the wilderness?
What's the sense of growing up when it's so much
easier to be childish?
Who needs your apologies when it doesn't stop the
pain
What's the sense of wiping my eyes when you're
the cause of the rain?
Who needs friends when they turn on you in the
end?
Who needs family when on not one of them you can
depend?
Who needs to breathe when the air stinks of death?
Who needs this life when you don't know how
much time is left

Who needs closure when it's just an excuse to hide
the feeling?
Who needs these thoughts when it prevents me from
healing?
Who needs it… Who needs it…Who needs it ….I do

## Will They Love Me Anyway?

Would they love me anyway despite my faults and
misfortunes? My wrong turns and deep valleys, my
every winding roads steep cliffs and mountains of
pain. Would they love me anyway accepting my
misled and ill-mannered thoughts, seeing my
charred battlefields of punished images. Would they
love me anyway? Over looking my ups and downs.
My now silent grounds. I told them, told them
everything surprisingly they love me anyway

## Two Weeks Too Late

I sat and contemplated
The reason you decided
To go, I sat and examined every
Facet of our time

I recalled you're unanswered
Request, each and every one
And what I should have done
Only a half a month too late

I found the closet that
Held all my broken promises
And all of my inattentive opinions
That she hid and stored away
Only fourteen days too late

I daydreamed of nights
I found company with
Anyone but her seeing effect
In my own self destructive cause
Only 336 hours too late

Segments of ignoring her
As if she never existed
Flashed in front of my eyes
The degeneration of my relationship
Only 20,160 minutes too late

A mere shell of the man
I was, my heart completely
And utterly useless
Better for grounded feed
Then inside my unworthy chest
Only two weeks too late

*I would like to take a moment to thank my loved*

*ones and those who supported me, my soon to be*

*wife Lara who stayed up on those late nights to read*

*my new poetry. She gave me the type of criticism*

*that I needed. My parents that have been there for*

*me throughout these 24 years thank you for your*

*parenting. There is no way that this thank you*

*would be complete without me mentioning my*

*grandmother Sarah who has been my backbone no*

*matter the weather, thank you so much and*

*I love you all.*